DISASTER STRIKES

Blizzard Night

DON'T MISS A MINUTE OF THESE HEART-STOPPING ADVENTURES!

Earthquake Shock

Tornado Alley

Blizzard Night

Volcano Blast

DISASTER STRIKES

Blizzard Night

by **MARLANE KENNEDY**

illustrated by
ERWIN MADRID

SCHOLASTIC INC.

**For Dave and Alice Kennedy,
whose little lakeside cabin in Michigan
helped to inspire this story.**

ISBN: 978-9-351-03815-3

First printing, November 2014

Designed by Nina Goffi

Printed and bound by MicroPrints (India), New Delhi
Reprinted by Scholastic India Pvt. Ltd., October 2015, June 2016, June 2018

CHAPTER 1

Ten-year-old Jayden Griffen sat quietly with an open book in his hands. He tried to ignore the nonstop chatter going on around him as a minivan carried him and most of the Walcott family toward a cabin in the Upper Peninsula of Michigan. The Walcotts were pretty much strangers to him. He'd met them only two weeks ago, and he wasn't quite sure what he thought of the boisterous bunch. Or what they thought of him. Unfortunately, he was just getting to the good part of his book when the argument started and tuning them out became a lost cause.

"Connor, could you change the radio station?" eleven-year-old Maggie asked from her seat next to Jayden. She heaved an irritated sigh. "I'm tired of country music." Leaning forward, she loomed over the front passenger seat to poke her brother.

Connor, who was ten just like Jayden, spun around. "I'm not putting on your boring pop music. I'd rather listen to fingernails scratching on a chalkboard."

"Dad!" Maggie whined, trying to get her father involved in the dispute.

Mr. Walcott responded by flicking the radio off.

"Dad!" Now it was Connor yelling at his father.

"Just trying to be fair," Mr. Walcott said cheerfully, unflustered by the bickering.

"You know, we wouldn't have this problem if you let us bring our phones and iPods," Maggie complained.

There was only one phone in the entire van and it belonged to Mr. Walcott. And he only brought it to keep in touch with his wife, who'd stayed behind in Cleveland, Ohio.

"The whole point of this trip is to spend quality family time with each other," Mr. Walcott said as he drove. "Once we get to the cabin we'll be so busy having fun you won't miss those things."

"All I know is that it better snow. A lot," Connor grumbled as he stared out the window. "There's barely enough on the ground to go snowmobiling. And it's the end of January. There should be at least a good foot or so!"

"Don't worry. It's supposed to start snowing right about the time we arrive," Mr. Walcott said. "The weatherman said we're in for around ten inches."

"The weatherman better be right," Connor said.

A soft snore came from the back of the van, causing Jayden to turn around and look. Six-year-old Rory, the youngest Walcott, was sound asleep. His chin lolled against his chest so all Jayden could see of him was a shock of poker-straight hair hanging over his face.

This family Jayden was traveling with happened to be his new foster family. And even though they bickered over dumb things like the radio station and snored in their sleep, Jayden thought the whole crew seemed like a good bunch. You could tell they really loved each other, and they were pretty nice to him.

But still, he couldn't help but feel out of place. It wasn't so much that he looked different from the rest of them. *All* the Walcott kids looked different from each other. In fact, Jayden actually looked more like his foster mom than any of the other kids did. But Connor, Maggie, and Rory had been adopted when they were tiny. They'd grown up in this tight-knit family. Mr. and Mrs. Walcott were the only mother and father they'd ever known.

Over the past two weeks, Jayden couldn't help but wonder why they even bothered with him in the first place. Their life seemed set. They were all successful in their own way. Mr. Walcott was a sports editor for a newspaper, and Mrs. Walcott was an architect. In fact, that is why Mrs. Walcott couldn't make the trip with them. She was in the middle of a project. The kids were great athletes. Maggie was a star gymnast, Connor a state-ranked wrestler, and Rory could do just about anything he wanted to with a soccer ball.

Jayden enjoyed sports well enough, but he was nothing special. He liked books more than playing on some team. So he worried about being accepted by the athletic Walcotts. He figured if he didn't do or say the wrong thing, maybe they'd let him stick around. But maybe that wasn't the best idea. He'd overheard a concerned Mrs. Walcott telling her husband that perhaps the winter trip would be a good "bonding" experience for them. "He's such a sweet, polite kid, but he seems sort of . . . aloof," she'd said.

He did feel pressure to open up, but it just wasn't that easy. It seemed safer, somehow, to sort of quietly float in the background.

He hoped they wouldn't regret taking him on the trip . . . taking him in. But he guessed that even if things didn't work out, at least he'd get to go on a cool vacation. Jayden had never really traveled much outside of Cleveland, so he was looking forward to seeing the type of wilderness he'd only read about in his books. From what he'd been told, the Walcotts' getaway cabin sat on a lake in a remote wooded area.

"You've never ridden a snowmobile before, have you?" Connor had turned around from the front seat to look at him.

Jayden shook his head.

"Man, you'll love it! It is so much fun!"

"Yeah, it's fun, but I like cross-country skiing better," Maggie said. "You really notice things. Often we'll see a deer or wild turkey. Sometimes even a bobcat or snowy owl!"

Jayden couldn't wait to try snowmobiling and skiing, but he was nervous about it, too. He hoped he did not look like a fool!

Actually, what he was looking forward to most of all was settling into a cozy spot by the fireplace and reading the books he'd brought along. There were three: one about a rain forest trek, one about rowing across the Atlantic, and the one he was currently reading, a book about an expedition to Mount Everest. Adventure stories were his favorite! *I may not have ever been anywhere exotic or done anything exciting,* he thought, *but reading about them is the next best thing.*

Another snore, this one louder, rumbled from the backseat. Everyone tried to contain themselves, but the giggles came bursting out. Even Jayden couldn't help but laugh as Rory finally stirred. "What's everyone laughing at?" he asked groggily. "Are we there yet?"

They'd been on the road since the crack of dawn, and now it was approaching mid-afternoon. It had been a long trip and Jayden had to admit he felt like asking the same question himself.

"Almost! Only an hour to go and we should be pulling into the driveway," Mr. Walcott said.

"Hey, look, it's starting to snow!" Connor pointed out the window.

The flakes were scattered and slowly drifting down.

"See, the weatherman wasn't lying," Mr. Walcott said. "Perfect timing, too. It's not supposed to hit hard until after we get to the cabin. Tomorrow morning we should be able to crank up the snowmobiles!"

Soon the van was filled with the playful banter of a family who knew one another well. Jayden couldn't think of anything to add, so he stared out the window at the deep woods rushing by in a blur. He didn't know the inside jokes, what he could tease them about. Would he ever know them that well? Would they ever know him that well? There were years of history among this family, and right now it felt overwhelming. With a shrug, he stuck his nose back in his book.

Before long, he lost track of time. Instead of riding in a van, he was climbing Mount Everest, weighed down by a backpack.

Exhausted. Frozen. The cold, still air quiet but for the sound of ragged breathing. The summit was tantalizingly close but seemed impossible to reach . . .

A bloodcurdling scream broke through the silent scene, tearing him away from his book. Jayden jerked his head up just in time to see Maggie's look of fear as a deer frantically leapt in front of the van.

Mr. Walcott swerved. The brakes squealed. And suddenly the van was tumbling down a steep hillside. Jayden's seat belt cut into his chest as his body was flung about. He didn't know whether he was facing up or down. The confusing whirl seemed to go on forever. Then a jolt stopped the van's fall with the crunching sound of impact.

CHAPTER 2

A stunned silence set upon the van. It took Jayden a few seconds to register what had just happened and to figure out they'd landed right side up. He really didn't want to look around at the wreckage, but as he caught his breath, he forced himself to. The van's front windshield was a spiderweb of shattered glass. There was also a crack along the front driver's side window, and the door was bashed in. Through the cracked glass, Jayden saw the rough brown shape of a large tree trunk — one that had ended their wild, dizzy descent.

Mr. Walcott was slumped against a deflated air bag, but then he slowly stirred, raising his head. "Is everyone okay?" he asked, his voice low and raspy. "Kids?" he demanded urgently, and Jayden saw the panic in his eyes.

Maggie moaned beside him. "I'm okay," she said. She rubbed her upper arm and grimaced. "Nothing's broken."

"I'm fine," Connor said as he pushed away from the air bag that had saved him from hitting the windshield head-on.

"Just got the wind knocked out of me!" he managed to croak.

"Me, too! I'm okay!" Rory tried to unbuckle himself from his seat in the very back and climb over the middle seats to be closer to his father, but couldn't manage it. He sported a bloody gash on his forehead.

"Rory!" Maggie shrieked. "Your head! You're bleeding!"

"No, I'm not," he said defiantly. But then he caught himself in the rearview mirror, which still stubbornly hung from the shattered windshield, and his eyes got wide. He looked down to see his shirt stained red.

"It's okay, Rory," Mr. Walcott said. "I promise. It's just a small cut. Foreheads bleed a lot. There's a first aid kit in the glove compartment. We'll fix you right up." Mr. Walcott leaned over to grab it, and his face twisted in agony. He struggled to inch closer to the passenger side. "My leg is trapped," he finally said. "It feels like it might be broken. Someone else is going to have to get the first aid kit."

Jayden peered over the seat at his foster father. The door beside him was crushed inward and the steering wheel was bent into his lap. Jayden didn't see any blood, but he suspected that Mr. Walcott's

leg might be hurt badly under the wreckage that trapped it.

Maggie and Connor must have realized it, too. "Dad? Dad? Dad?" Connor repeated over and over as Maggie began to sob hysterically.

"Stop!" Mr. Walcott yelled. "I'm okay. I'm not the first person in the world to break their leg. I promise I'm okay. I promise we'll *all* be okay."

Connor and Maggie grew quiet, but both still looked wild-eyed and desperate.

"Jayden, you're the calmest right now. Get the first aid kit out of the glove compartment for Rory. Wipe his cut with antiseptic and then stretch a butterfly bandage across it. Okay?" Mr. Walcott asked.

"Yes, sir." Jayden nodded solemnly. Connor made room so Jayden could lean over the front seat and grab the kit from the glove box.

Rory looked at his foster brother with huge eyes as Jayden tended to the little boy's injury. Jayden could tell he was scared. Rory winced when Jayden applied the antiseptic but bit his lip in an attempt to be brave. Jayden gave him an encouraging smile. Mr. Walcott was right. His cut wasn't as bad as it first seemed. It was already starting to clot by the time he applied the bandage to it.

"Now what do we do?" Maggie asked. She seemed much calmer now, and Connor was more composed, too.

"Let me find my phone," her father said. "The reception can be spotty here, but hopefully we'll get through to 911." Mr. Walcott dug around in the crushed side door beside him, and after a few moments announced, "I found it!" But when he pulled it out, it looked as crushed as the car door. He fiddled with it, but before long he sighed with disappointment. "It's no use. It's too busted to work."

By now the snow was coming more quickly. It was no longer a smattering of flakes, but a steady flow softly falling around them.

"Maybe someone will see us from the road," Maggie said.

"I don't think so." Mr. Walcott shook his head. "We landed too far down the hillside for anyone to notice. Besides, there aren't that many people up here this time of year. And with the snowstorm forecasted for tonight, anyone who is at their cabin will probably stay put."

"Just how far are we from the lake?" Jayden asked.

"About two miles straight down this road," Mr. Walcott said. "When you first get there, you'll notice a few cabins. Ours is about another mile down the loop that goes around the lake."

"What time is it? About three o'clock,

right?" Connor asked. "There's still a few hours of daylight left." The shock of the accident had worn off, and he no longer looked like a frightened child. He had his game face on — a warrior look that Jayden imagined he probably used on his wrestling opponents. "I can go get help. If I knock on enough cabin doors someone is bound to be around. If worst comes to worst, I can break inside. Only to use the phone, of course," Connor said, breaking into a smile Jayden hadn't seen in a while. "I doubt our neighbors will mind."

Mr. Walcott frowned. Jayden guessed he didn't want Connor to leave. *But what choice do we have?* Jayden thought. *If we all stay in the van and no one notices us for days, how will we survive? Someone has to go get help.*

Mr. Walcott must have come to the same conclusion. The frown disappeared and he nodded at his son. "Just follow the road, Connor. Shouldn't take but an hour — maybe less — to reach the lake and cabins. Your winter gear is packed in one of the suitcases in the trunk, so go ahead and suit up as quickly as you can. But I don't want you to go alone . . ."

Before Mr. Walcott could finish, Jayden piped up. "I'll go with him!" The force with which he said it surprised even Jayden, but he felt compelled to help. It was better to keep busy and do something — anything — than just sit and helplessly wait.

CHAPTER 3

"I'll go, too, Dad," Maggie said.

"No, you stay here with me and Rory," Mr. Walcott replied. "Jayden and Connor can manage."

"I'm going," Maggie said defiantly. "I'm the oldest kid. And you can't stop me."

The two locked eyes for a moment in a silent battle.

"Really, Dad, you *can't* stop me. You've

got a broken leg, remember?" Maggie's sternness eased into a grin. "You can't exactly chase me down, can you?"

Mr. Walcott gave her a scolding look, but relented. "Okay, you can go with them. But I need you three to stay together. Promise me you'll look after one another."

Jayden, Connor, and Maggie nodded.

"Maggie and I have walked two miles before, Dad. It really isn't a big deal," Connor told him.

"Well, I want you all to be prepared. Put on all your snow gear — that includes gloves and boots, Connor — and take some of the leftover snacks we had for the drive here." Mr. Walcott turned to face Jayden and Maggie, but suddenly he caught his breath and his face contorted in pain. He quickly twisted back toward the damaged dashboard, and Jayden winced in sympathy. That leg must kill. Jayden thought about how he would feel if he were in Mr. Walcott's place. How awful it would be to be stranded with a broken bone. They'd need to hurry to get Mr. Walcott some relief! He was surprised to feel a surge of loyalty and fondness toward the man who had only recently become his foster dad.

Maggie climbed to the rear bench seat and lifted out three suitcases. After an awkward few minutes of struggling to get dressed in the cramped van, Jayden and the oldest two Walcott kids were ready to face the elements. All were bundled in thick puffy coats and pants, gloves, knit caps, and boots they'd brought for snowmobiling. They each stuffed their pockets with small Mylar bags of Goldfish crackers and as many Jolly Ranchers as they could fit.

"Take care of Daddy," Maggie told her little brother.

Rory nodded solemnly.

"We'll be fine," Mr. Walcott said. "I'll turn on the engine every once in a while for heat. It still seems to be working. And we've got the rest of the snacks to tide us over till help comes."

Connor and Maggie scooted out of the van, but just as Jayden was about to follow, something made him stop. He remembered seeing something in the first aid kit that might be useful: a book of matches. His thoughts went to a vivid scene in the book he'd been reading when the van crashed — a half-frozen expedition group climbing Mount Everest gathered around a fire at a base camp near the summit. He fumbled around and found the book of matches, shoving them quickly into his pocket.

"What's taking so long?" Connor asked, irritated.

"Nothing," Jayden said. He hopped out of the van. He felt a little silly for thinking about his book when Mr. Walcott was in pain. And, really, why would they need matches for a little two-mile hike anyway? He had let his imagination carry him away. They weren't exactly climbing the world's highest mountain like the characters he'd been reading about. He gave a sheepish grin to apologize for slowing them down but didn't bother explaining.

Connor just shrugged and rolled his eyes.

The three kids waved good-bye to Rory and Mr. Walcott and then began to scramble up the embankment.

They were only halfway up the hillside when Jayden began to pant. Climbing in snow pants, a heavy coat, and boots wasn't easy. Connor and Maggie were in better shape than he was and reached the top first. They stood waiting for him, and Jayden wondered if maybe he should have stayed behind with Mr. Walcott and Rory. He didn't want to slow them down. But he was here now, and he figured once they reached the road it would get easier.

And it did. As the three kids walked down the road, Jayden was able to catch his breath. The snow was really coming down now, and soon the deep woods around them sagged underneath thick piles of the stuff.

Maggie and Connor were quiet. Probably worried about their father. *It must be nice, in a way, to worry about family,* Jayden thought. He'd been a foster kid for half his life. For the first few years, he'd lived with a kind elderly couple until health problems prevented them from keeping him. Then he'd stayed at a large group home with lots of other foster kids. It'd been loud all the time. And no one ever seemed to stick around very long. And now the Walcotts had taken him in. He'd always been treated just fine wherever he was, but he longed for a place that was truly home and a real family.

The late-afternoon sun slanted onto the landscape, making everything from the tree branches to the road sparkle. Big flakes of snow melted on his nose and caught on his eyelashes. It was peaceful and still. Really beautiful, actually. Jayden had spent his whole life in the city and had never seen

anything like it before. Snowfall in the city was different than out here. For one thing, it usually got dirty as soon as it fell! Here there was nothing to spoil it. He walked alongside Connor and Maggie and let a sense of wonder wash over him.

Nearly thirty minutes later, the wind picked up. It bent the trees and whipped snow into Jayden's face in icy blasts. The sky turned gloomy and dark. What had been a comfortable walk started to become miserable. All three kids popped their coat hoods over their heads to block out the chill.

"Thank goodness we're over halfway to the lake," Maggie said, breaking the long silence. "I'm getting cold."

"Me, too," said Connor. "But it won't be long now."

Yet as soon as the words were spoken, the snow began to fall in blinding sheets. Jayden couldn't see anything but whiteness. It was disorienting, and he couldn't help stumbling. Maggie and Connor had to be right beside him, but he felt totally alone in the stark nothingness that suddenly enveloped him.

CHAPTER 4

Maggie called out to the boys, her voice drawing them closer until all three were finally huddled together. They stood still; almost afraid to move for fear of losing one another again in the swirl of white that swallowed everything. The snow was falling fast and furiously from every direction.

"What do we do now?" Maggie shouted over the howling wind. "Who knows how long this blizzard will last! We'll freeze to death just standing here!"

"We could lock arms and keep walking," Jayden shouted back. "That way we won't lose each other again."

"Yes, let's do that. We have to keep going!" Connor urged.

With Maggie in the middle, and arms firmly intertwined, they began the trek to the lake cabins once again, taking cautious steps without knowing exactly what was in front of them. Everything around them had vanished. Jayden thought about how strange it was that the bright-white storm was just as difficult to negotiate as the pitch-black night.

After a few minutes Jayden tripped and

almost fell. The snow-covered ground seemed different here. Rougher. "I think we've wandered off the road," he yelled.

"This way!" Connor tugged them in another direction.

But still the ground beneath their feet did not even out.

Connor led as they pushed their way through the blowing snow. Jayden wondered how they'd ever find the road again. But before panic could rise in his chest, his thoughts were interrupted.

"Ouch!" Connor cried. "I just ran into something." He steadied himself against the obstacle that blocked their path. "A tree, I think. And its branches are sharp. Be careful!"

They soldiered on, but it was only a matter of seconds until they smacked into another tree. And another. Still they struggled onward, not daring to let go of each other's arms for fear the storm would separate and devour them. For all Jayden knew they could be walking in circles. But what else could they do? The damp coldness was starting to get to him, yet he knew moving was keeping them all warm.

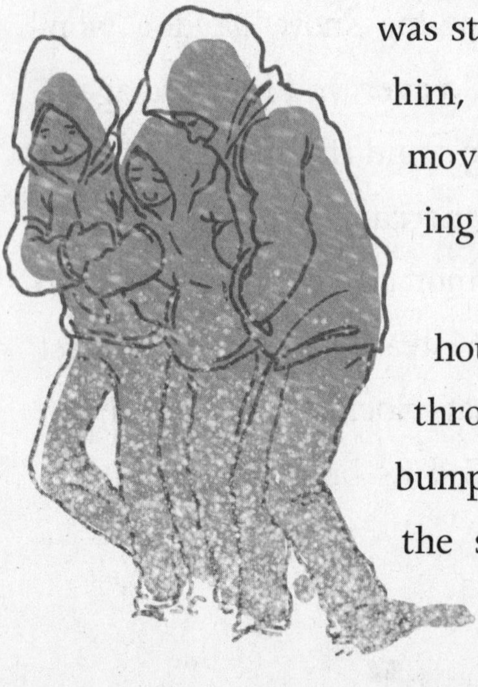

After nearly an hour of stumbling through brush and bumping into trees, the snowfall began to ease. It was still coming down at a steady pace, but they were finally able to make out what was around them. And even though it was quite obvious they were lost in the middle of the woods, Jayden was thrilled to be able to finally see Maggie's and Connor's faces.

The three kids stopped and stared at one another, smiling with relief.

"Does anyone see a clearing in the trees? A big open space that'd tell us where the road is — or even the lake, if we're close enough?" Connor asked.

They craned their necks to try to get their bearings, but in every direction, all that could be seen was snow-covered woods.

"It'll be dark soon. And the temperature has dropped. We should find shelter for the night while there's still some light left," Jayden said. "We can continue on in the morning." He flashed back to a harrowing scene in his Everest book, where a climber had almost frozen to death from hypothermia but was saved by tunneling into the snow to protect himself from the wind and trap his body heat. Here, though, the snow just wasn't deep enough yet to burrow into. Maybe they could find a hollow tree for shelter. His face already felt numb. *I could start a fire with the matches I brought,* he thought. *I bet Maggie and Connor will be glad I tagged along.* But before he could open his mouth to mention it, Maggie spoke.

"No!" she said. "W-w-we can't be that far away! In another tw-twenty minutes or so, we could be there. We should keep going."

"I agree with Maggie," Connor said. "The sun hasn't gone down yet and if we reach help soon, then by midnight Dad will have his leg in a cast and we can all spend the night in our own cabin. That's a heck of a lot better than huddling up here in the woods."

Jayden knew he was outnumbered, so he didn't argue. Plus he wanted to help their dad just as much as they did. He just hoped they were right. "So which way do we go?" he asked.

The sky was too overcast to see where the sun was setting. There was no clue which way was north, south, east, or west.

"Let's head that way." Connor pointed. "It is to the right of our footsteps so at least we won't be going backward." He started walking, while Maggie and Jayden trailed behind.

By now, Jayden was so stiff with cold that it was hard to move, but he forced each step, hoping it would take him closer to safety. And warmth. He swore he could feel the chill all the way to his bones. His cheeks began to prickle and itch, his chest ached with every breath.

They had only walked for about ten minutes when he noticed Maggie's shoulders were shaking. She was shivering badly, and had her arms wrapped around her sides. He watched as her steps grew unsteady and wobbly.

"Maggie! Are you okay?" he asked. He hurried a few steps to catch up to her.

She looked dazed. "Yeth." Then she mumbled something else, but her voice trembled and her speech was too slurred to make out.

Jayden knew she most definitely wasn't okay.

CHAPTER 5

"Stop!" Jayden called out to Connor. "Hey, hold up a minute!"

"What?" Connor turned back toward Jayden and Maggie. His face was twisted in frustration. Jayden guessed he didn't want their mission interrupted when it was so important.

"There's something wrong with Maggie," Jayden told him.

"N-n-n-no. N-n-n-not," Maggie said through chattering teeth. "I'm-m-m ok-k-k-kay. Let's-s-s g-g-go."

Connor gasped. "Maggie! Your lips . . . they're blue! And you're shivering like crazy!"

"We need to get her warm and find something to shelter her from the wind. Now. She looks like she might be getting hypothermia," Jayden said, trying to make his voice as firm as possible. He'd put up a fight this time if he had to. No way would he let them travel on. He remembered the hypothermia scene in his book, and it looked like Maggie had all of the same symptoms. "She's too cold! And she's losing heat faster than her body can produce it." He shook his head. "Trust me. It's dangerous!"

"Okay. But where on earth are we going to find shelter out here?" By now Connor had wrapped an arm around his sister protectively and rubbed her shoulders to help warm her.

"I'm s-s-s-sor-r-r-ry." Maggie struggled to get the words out. "It's-s-s-s all my fault. We wil-l-l-l be s-s-s-stuck out here."

"Hush," Jayden said, cutting her off. "It's only a matter of time before Connor and I have symptoms just like yours. It's getting colder out here by the minute." The snowfall had lightened enough so that in the distance he could make out a rocky hillside. Snow had begun to drift and pile along the outcropping. "Maybe we can dig out a hole along those rocky crags over there. It looks like it's only about five minutes away."

This time he got no argument. Jayden was relieved. If he or Connor came down with hypothermia, too, there was no way they'd survive the night. Maggie hadn't shown any severe symptoms yet — like confusion, hallucinations, or acting irrationally. But he knew if they wandered around hopelessly lost and crazed, it would not end well. If they could stay warm until morning, perhaps the weather would be better for their hike to get help. Plus they'd be able to see the sun rise so they could get a sense of which direction to go.

With Maggie in the middle, and the boys hovering on either side of her to keep the wind and cold at bay, the group made their way through the woods to the rocky hillside.

When they came within feet of the area, Connor grew excited. "Hey, look, isn't that a cave?"

Jayden spotted the darkened hole in the hillside. They wouldn't have to dig a tunnel through snow to make shelter. A safe place out of the wind and snow was right there waiting for them!

"It's a cave! It is!" Jayden could hardly believe their good fortune. The cave looked to be about four feet high and about the same wide, but the wind had created a snowdrift near the entrance that would need to be cleared. He could probably kick a path through it for them in a matter of minutes. "Hold on to Maggie," Jayden told Connor, "while I get the snow out of the way."

Though he felt stiff and achy, the excitement of knowing something Maggie and Connor didn't spurred him on. He had the book of matches in his pocket! Soon they'd be sitting near a fire. Thank goodness he thought to bring them after all! He quickly set to work shoving aside about two feet of drifted snow.

Once done, he stooped over and made his way inside the cave, waving for Connor and Maggie to follow him. It was dim inside, but it looked plenty deep enough for the three of them to cozy up. He was in such a hurry to get Maggie inside that he didn't notice the dip in the ground until it was too late.

As he fell, he reached out with his gloved hands to catch himself. But the landing wasn't as hard as he'd expected. In fact, it was kind of soft. And surprisingly warm. His face brushed up against something furry, and he froze in shock.

The soft lump he landed on stirred.

CHAPTER 6

Jayden's first instinct was to scream and run. It took all the strength he could muster to remain still. A scene from a book he'd read nearly a year ago came flooding back to him. A boy had accompanied his father, a zoologist, on a trip to study caribou in the Alaskan wilderness. The boy wandered off and eventually came upon an angry mama bear. He knew not to run and it saved his life. There is no way to outrun a bear. They're faster, hands down. And running makes the bear think you're prey.

Slowly and quietly, Jayden eased his way up to his feet. He didn't want to rouse the bear. With luck it would drift back into its winter slumber, totally unaware that its space had been invaded.

"Holy cow!" Connor gasped from behind when he noticed the large creature inhabiting the cave. "Run!" He spun around and reached for his sister's hand so he could drag her along in his attempt to escape.

Jayden grabbed Connor by the arm, twisting him back before he could flee. "Don't!" He looked at Connor as gravely as possible and spoke in a low, soft voice. "He'll go after you and he'll win."

Just then, the bear emitted a low grumbling moan and lumbered to its feet, sniffing the air and pawing the ground. Connor looked unsure about the advice Jayden had just given him, but did as he was told.

"Back away slowly," Jayden whispered. "And whatever you do, don't look him in the eye."

Maggie seemed awestruck by the majestic beast. She took a staggering step forward toward the bear. *She doesn't know any better,* Jayden thought. *The hypothermia is getting to her. She's totally out of it.*

Connor, realizing his sister was not to be trusted in her current state, scooped her up into his arms and slowly began to inch backward. Jayden followed as quietly as he could. He kept his eyes firmly on the ground. Slowly but surely the three kids made their way out of the cave.

At first it appeared the bear might remain inside. But then it, too, cautiously emerged from the cave and approached them. Fear poured through Jayden. He stared at the huge clawed paws that padded

the snow-covered ground. He tried not to think of the damage they could do.

"I think we should play dead," Connor whispered, his voice barely loud enough to be heard.

Jayden remembered that the boy from his book had tried that, and the bear had left him alone. But later, the boy's father had told him how lucky he was that it was a grizzly bear he'd met. That if it had been a hungry black bear going after him, he wouldn't have survived using that trick. And Jayden knew that grizzlies didn't live in Michigan. This one had to be a black bear. And if it decided it was hungry, they'd just make things easier for it by playing dead.

"No. Keep going. Trust me," Jayden murmured back.

The snow was deep enough to make walking backward difficult. Jayden dared a direct peek at the bear. The beast had come to a stop, and though his body remained still, he swung his head back and forth anxiously as if trying to decide what to do.

When they were about sixty feet away from the bear, Jayden breathed a sigh of relief and turned toward Maggie and Connor. "I think we're in the clear," he told them.

But he'd spoken too soon. The bear snorted. It pounded the ground. Jayden looked back just in time to catch a sudden flash of black.

The bear was charging right at them.

CHAPTER 7

"Watch out!" Connor dropped to the ground and covered Maggie with his body in a desperate attempt to protect her.

Jayden stepped in front of them. He stretched his arms over his head, waving them frantically so he'd appear as large and ferocious as possible. He shouted, "Go away! Get out of here!" The words formed white puffs in the frigid air. He knew their only hope was to call the bear's bluff. If it thought they were fiercer and meaner, maybe Jayden could scare it off. But if the bear wasn't bluffing . . .

The bear came, chuffing and huffing, bounding straight for him.

Jayden's muscles tensed. He braced himself for what was to come. "Go away!" he roared one last time.

And just as quickly as it had taken

off, the bear abruptly stopped. It stared at Jayden a moment, clicking its jaws nervously, then turned away and ambled back to the safety of its cave.

Once the bear had disappeared inside, a wave of immense relief made Jayden feel like slumping to the ground next to Connor and Maggie. But he collected himself and gently bent over the two of them instead. "It's okay, now," he said. "I scared it off. It didn't mean us any harm. It just felt threatened, that's all."

Connor sat up and looked around. "Is it really gone?" he asked. But Jayden didn't answer. Maggie still lay on the ground. She was shivering and breathing fast. She looked ghostly.

All of a sudden neither boy was worried about the bear anymore.

Connor stood, picked her up, and held her close. "We need to get her warm. Somehow, someway we need to get her warm."

Jayden glanced around. The snow was still coming down, and now that the panic over being mauled had faded, he was keenly aware of how cold it was. To his right, he noticed several enormous boulders leaning against one another about a quarter of a mile away. It looked like there was a little sheltered space below where they met. "Over there!" he pointed. "Can you carry her there?"

Maggie lifted her head from her brother's shoulder. "I c-c-can walk," she said.

"We can get there quicker if I carry you," Connor said firmly.

For once, she didn't argue. And it turned out Connor was right. Maggie had the tiny frame of a gymnast and Connor had the solid build of a wrestler. In fact, Jayden had a hard time keeping up with Connor's quick, sure steps.

By the time they reached the boulders, Jayden himself had begun to shake from the cold. He did his best to ignore it and made quick work of scooping and kicking snow from the triangle-shaped tunnel that the boulders created. Once cleared, Connor set Maggie down inside the makeshift shelter and huddled close to her.

"I have matches, but they're no good

without tinder," Jayden said. His first foster family, the elderly couple, often built bonfires on summer evenings, and Jayden knew a bit about what it took to get a fire going. He stood outside the tunnel and looked around.

"You've got matches?" Connor's jaw dropped. "Where'd you get them?"

"I grabbed them from the first aid kit before we left your dad and Rory." Jayden felt useful. It was a good feeling. Actually, a great one. Connor looked at him with such admiration that even though his cheeks felt like ice cubes, he wondered if he was blushing.

"Nice work, bro! Let's get a fire going and warm Maggie up." Connor smiled.

"Yeah, but like I said, first I've got to find something dry we can light. Any idea what I could use?"

"What about that cluster of pine trees over there." Connor peeked out and gestured. "When we come up here in the fall, there's usually a carpet of dry dead needles littering the ground."

"I'll dig under the snow and see what I can find. You stay close to Maggie and keep her warm," Jayden told him. By now the sun had almost set. There wasn't much time left before nightfall. He needed to get the fire started before it was too late to see what he was doing.

Jayden scrambled over to the pine trees and was able to find some needles under the snow. He took off his knit cap and filled it with the thin red-brown shafts. The wind whipped sharply through his curly hair and nipped at his uncovered ears. He pulled loose bark from a few trees and picked up a few sticks poking up from the snow-covered ground. Arms full, he brought the spoils of his hunt back to the boulders and headed out for more. Then he went in search of larger pieces of wood that could keep a fire going. He found a fallen tree that was long dead and snapped the branches off by the armload.

By the time he had a ring of the needles, bark, sticks, and branches built at the entrance of the tunnel, his entire head was numb. He couldn't control the shivering that overtook his body.

The tunnel was cramped, with barely room for the three of them, but Jayden figured that would work to their advantage when it came to getting warm. He took off his gloves, and despite stiff, frozen fingers, he managed to dig the book of matches out of his pocket. He struck one match and held it with a shaking hand to a clump of pine needles. The match flared, but went out without igniting anything.

Connor moaned in disappointment.

The next match went out, too. *What if I go through this whole book of matches and don't get a fire started?* Jayden was growing frustrated. And worried. But the third

time was the charm, and soon the pine needles began to glow orange. The flame grew steadily as Jayden rearranged the branches and sticks.

The warmth from the small fire felt good on his face and hands. "Bring Maggie closer," he told Connor.

And so the kids settled in for the night. Since there wasn't much room, they had Maggie sit closest to the fire. The other two snuggled in behind her. In time, Maggie's shivering eased and her cheeks began to look pinker. Jayden stopped shivering, too. His face and ears tingled as the numbness wore off. No one really felt warm or comfortable, but at least the cold wasn't so painful.

It was pitch-black outside, but the fire illuminated the still falling snow. They ate a dinner of Goldfish and Jolly Ranchers without talking much. Connor reached out into the snow and scooped a handful to his mouth.

"Don't!" Jayden barked.

"Why not? I'm thirsty! We have to be dehydrated by now. We need water and snow is basically water, isn't it?"

"Eating frozen snow will lower your body temperature. It can make hypothermia worse. Which wouldn't be good considering the situation we're in."

"So what are we supposed to do?" Connor snapped. "Die of thirst instead of freezing to death?"

"Hey, I know!" Maggie said. Jayden noticed that she was no longer stuttering or slurring her speech. She held out an empty Goldfish bag and said, "Can't we fill these with snow and hold it close enough to the fire to melt?"

Within minutes the three kids were drinking from Goldfish bags. They had shelter, a fire, a bit of food, and something to quench their thirst. They were okay. For now.

"So how did you know all that stuff about hypothermia? And what to do about facing a bear?" Connor asked. "Are you a genius or something?"

Jayden laughed. "No, I just read adventure books. Lots of them."

As the night grew on, Jayden began to hold his first real conversation with his foster brother and sister. They talked. They really talked.

Maggie and Connor told funny stories about school and their friends.

"I should invite some of the guys over soon so you can get to know them better," Connor said. "Fred can burp nursery rhymes like 'Row, Row, Row Your Boat,' and Kyle can impersonate anyone. Even me! He cracks me up."

"Oh, please, no! Fred and Kyle are so annoying!" Maggie said. She rolled her eyes, but she was grinning like she enjoyed their antics, too.

"Yeah, like Jayden would rather be around your giggly friends," Connor said.

"Well, I bet Lily could outbelch Fred anytime!"

"She probably could!" Connor laughed.

Jayden shared stories, too. First about kind Mr. and Mrs. Sheffield, who had cared for him. Then about the busy, hectic life he experienced later on in the home filled with many foster kids. They were good stories about pleasant things, but still there was a tinge of sadness to Jayden's voice. "A lot of times, just when I'd get to be good friends with someone in the group home, they'd move on for one reason or another," he said.

"That must have been tough," Maggie said.

Jayden shrugged and stared at the fire. He longed for a real family and a real home. He didn't share this longing with Maggie and Connor, but they seemed to be able to sense this and grew quiet.

It was just as well. It was late and they needed their sleep. As Jayden finally drifted off, he thought about how this freak storm had given him a gift of sorts. He'd gotten to know Connor and Maggie so much better without the distractions of snowmobiles and adventure novels than he would have at the cabin. Still, as much as he'd enjoyed the past couple of hours by the warm fire with them, he hoped that the morning wouldn't bring another blizzard. He couldn't think of anything worse.

CHAPTER 8

Fortunately, Jayden awoke to bright sunshine streaming into the tunnel between the boulders. And no falling snow! As he stirred and stretched, he noticed that the fire had almost burned out. But at least it'd kept the snow from drifting too close. Further out, the snow looked deep.

Maggie and Connor groggily opened their eyes as Jayden got to his feet.

"I'm going to peek outside," Jayden told them.

Out in the open, the air was still. Jayden guessed the temperature must be in the mid-thirties. Not bad. The sky was blue and the snow reflected sunlight in brilliant bursts, making him squint. He took a few more steps away from the boulders into snow that practically came up to his knees. It would be difficult to walk through, but since the weather had calmed down, he'd take it.

The smoldering fire still gave off enough warmth that the kids could melt and drink some more water. Despite the hunger that invaded their empty stomachs, it would have to do for breakfast.

Soon they'd packed their few belongings and crept outside the leaning boulders, peering in every direction to survey their surroundings. "Which way do we go?" Maggie asked.

"The sun rises in the east. We need to go farther north to reach the lake cabins." Connor pointed, then grinned. "Using the sun as a compass is one of the few things I learned from the year I was in Scouts. I'm regretting not paying more attention to

our troop leader, but I think I can at least get us going in the right direction."

Even with the sun as a guide, finding those cabins in the middle of nowhere is going to be like hunting for a needle in a haystack, Jayden thought.

Maggie must have been having the same worries. "What if we wander around all day and don't find any help, and we just get even more lost, and it gets dark and freezing cold again?" She suddenly looked scared.

"Staying put won't help," Connor told her. "No one even knows to come looking for us. Plus Rory and Dad are depending on us. We need to keep going. Especially since the weather is good right now."

Jayden thought of his injured foster dad back in the van. Every passing minute must seem like an eternity to him. Once the blizzard started, he must have been worried sick about them. And by now he'd probably guessed that they were lost, since help never arrived. He could only imagine how badly Mr. Walcott's leg must hurt. "Connor's right," Jayden told Maggie. "We've got to at least try."

The going was slow. Every step through the deep snow took intense effort. But the sun continued to keep them warm and they trudged on. After a while, Jayden even felt like he might be sweating a bit so he unzipped his coat.

A good while later — it must have

been around noon since the sun was directly overhead — the ground started to slope down. It made walking a bit easier and they picked up their pace. Soon Connor spotted a large clearing in the distance.

"Hey, there aren't any trees over there! That's got to be the lake!" he shouted.

Adrenaline kicked in and now they were moving even faster, almost high-stepping through the snow.

"It *is* the lake! It has to be the lake!" Maggie exclaimed as they drew closer. "I see a cabin! And look, there's smoke coming from the chimney! Someone is home!"

Maggie pointed at a small wooded finger

of land that jutted into the clearing. And sure enough, Jayden saw a cabin nestled among the trees.

"I know that cabin," Connor said. "I think we passed it when we were boating last summer. It's on the opposite side of the lake from ours."

Soon the kids made it down to the shoreline, where the trees stopped and only a smooth coat of snow spread out before them. Jayden thought the cabin ahead was the most beautiful sight he'd ever seen. It meant everything would be okay. It meant they wouldn't have to spend another night in the woods. That Mr. Walcott and Rory would be rescued. That none of them would freeze or starve to death. It was just a matter of time before they'd all be safe and sound.

Maggie looked over at him and grinned, her face flushed with joy.

Jayden started to grin back, when all of a sudden something cracked beneath his feet. The unmistakable sound of ice splintering under the snow. He saw Maggie's expression change from one of delight to sheer terror.

They weren't following the shoreline, they were standing on the lake itself. And the ice wasn't frozen solid.

The cracking grew louder. Before Jayden could react, his footing gave way and his body plunged into ice-cold water. The sun disappeared as he sank into the murky darkness. With all of the energy he could muster, he kicked his legs until his head broke the water's surface, and he gasped for air. He thrashed around, trying to get a grip on the edge of the ice, but his heavy coat and boots weighed him down and he sunk into the frigid waters once again.

CHAPTER 9

Jayden held his breath. He struggled out of his gloves and his waterlogged coat before popping back up to the surface again. He sucked air into his lungs as he tried to tread water, but his snow pants and boots made it difficult.

"Get off the ice! Now! Go get help at the cabin!" Connor screamed at his sister.

Jayden caught a glimpse of Maggie standing in shocked silence on the perilous ice before finally scrambling away, the ice crackling and moaning until she disappeared from his line of sight.

He went under again and fought his way back up. When he managed to get his head above water he saw Connor lying on a shelf of snow and ice right above him with his hand extended. "Grab on," he said.

Jayden reached up with his frozen, numb hand and Connor latched on to him.

"Just keep still. Let me pull you up," Connor said. Slowly Connor began to inch backward across the snow. He grimaced, the strain of Jayden's weight evident on his face. *Creak!* The ice he was laying on shifted beneath him.

What if they both were to go in?

Jayden rose a few inches out of the water

with Connor's help and grasped the frozen edge of the hole to help hoist himself the rest of the way out. All his energy spent, he lay down on the ice, panting through chattering teeth, unsure what they should do next. He felt weak, and though he wanted to jump up and run for the shore, he knew that probably wasn't a good idea.

"I think we should crawl," Connor said. "The ice might not give if our weight is spread out."

Jayden nodded. They carefully soldier-crawled their way toward the tree line,

inch by inch. Each time the ice groaned underneath his body, Jayden shut his eyes and clenched his fists.

Once they reached the trees, Connor helped Jayden to his feet.

Up ahead, Jayden caught sight of Maggie slogging through the deep snow as fast as she could.

Connor cupped his hands and shouted, "Maggie! He's out! We're coming!" He took off his coat and wrapped it around Jayden. It did little to stop the deep-down cold Jayden felt in his bones. He was shivering violently, but seeing how close they were to the cabin made him stumble forward. Connor put his arm around him to help support his shaky steps.

Maggie waited for them to catch up to her and then she, too, wrapped a protective arm around Jayden to help him along. "I'm so glad you're okay. I thought" — her voice caught — "I thought you were going to drown before I could get help. I was so scared."

When they finally reached the front door of the cabin, it was all Jayden could do not to collapse in a frozen heap. Maggie pounded on the door. "Help! Is anybody home? Someone, please help us!"

The door swung open and a surprised gentleman with gray hair and a beard greeted them. "Opal!" he called and was soon joined by an older woman with a kind, round face.

"Gus, these kids look colder than an

Arctic ice-cream cone!" Opal said. "Come in, come in!" Opal ushered the kids inside without question.

But as the kids shivered in the hall, the story came spilling out. The accident. Mr. Walcott's broken leg and how he and Rory were stranded down a ravine only a few miles away. Their night in the blizzard. Jayden's fall into the lake.

"Opal, call an ambulance, and I'll take these two in the truck to find their father and brother," Gus said. He then spoke to Maggie and Connor. "We're closer than emergency service, so I'll see what we can do to make your dad comfortable until the ambulance arrives. We can at least bring him some water and something to eat. The roads were bad this morning, but I heard the plow go by about an hour ago. Should be able to get to them in just a few minutes."

Opal nodded and Gus left with Maggie and Connor. When she was done making the phone call for emergency help, Opal turned her attention to a dripping and damp Jayden. "Let's get you out of those wet clothes, dear," she said.

Jayden was given a fluffy towel, a flannel shirt, and pair of tan pants and shown to the bathroom. As he dried off and changed into the clothes, he instantly felt better. The shirt and pants must have belonged to Gus — they were way too big. But Jayden didn't mind. They were dry and toasty!

When he emerged, Opal directed him to a big overstuffed chair by a crackling fire. "Sit here. Let me get you some hot chocolate. And maybe a sandwich. I imagine you're hungry after spending the night in the woods. Do you like ham and cheese?"

Jayden smiled. "That sounds terrific. Thanks."

Though it wasn't gourmet or anything, the hot chocolate and ham and cheese sandwich Opal brought him seemed like the best meal he'd had in his entire life. Nothing had ever tasted so sweet and delicious!

The fire glowed and snapped, and Jayden sank deeper into the soft chair. An overwhelming feeling of gratitude poured through him, warming him just as much as the fire. He thought about how the trip had started out. How he'd been concerned about fitting in with the Walcotts and how he'd felt so awkward around them. But during the night, he hadn't worried once about whether Maggie or Connor liked him or not. That'd been the last thing on his mind. Like his new foster brother and sister, he was too busy trying to survive.

And survive they had. By staying together and depending on one another, they'd made it through the blizzard night.

CHAPTER 10

Jayden was flying fast enough that the wind stung his cheeks. The morning sun was strong and bounced off the snow, but his tinted goggles helped with the glare. And his new winter coat and snow pants kept him warm.

"Can I go faster?" he shouted. This was the last day of their winter getaway, and he wanted to make the most of it.

"Yes!" Mr. Walcott yelled from behind. "You're doing great! Just like a pro!"

Jayden was driving the two-seater snowmobile while Mr. Walcott sat behind him. His foster dad had his lower left leg in a cast, but it didn't slow him down at all during the week they'd spent in the Upper Peninsula. The break in the bone was simple and clean, and once set, he was able to do everything he'd planned during the trip. He just moved a bit slower!

Jayden revved the engine and tried to catch up to Connor, who was bounding through the snow up ahead on a smaller snowmobile. Maggie and Rory waited patiently for their turn, as they would soon switch off.

Jayden was having the time of his life! He couldn't quite believe he was driving a snowmobile. A snowmobile! He drove over a small bump, and suddenly he and his foster dad were airborne for a second or two. Jayden felt totally free. He laughed into the crisp, chilly air.

An hour later, the family gathered in the kitchen of the cabin for lunch. It was their last meal before heading back to Ohio. Mr. Walcott had made chili the night before and they ate the leftovers, piling their bowls with crackers, cheese, and sour cream. Jayden thought the chili tasted even better than it did the previous night — the spicy warmth was perfect after spending the morning outside in the cold.

Jayden looked around the cabin as he ate. Despite the rough start to the trip, he loved it here. The cabin was small and nothing fancy, but it was cozy. Wood beams lined the ceiling, throw rugs were scattered about, and a well-worn plaid couch faced a stone fireplace. When he wasn't busy having fun in the great outdoors, he'd snuggled into the couch by the fire and read his adventure novels.

"I can't believe it's time to go home already," Jayden told the others. "I had an awesome time. Well, except for how the trip started out, of course!"

"I'm so glad you were with us," Mr. Walcott said. He smiled at Jayden as he blew on a big spoonful of chili.

"Me, too," Connor said. "If you hadn't come along, Jayden, we wouldn't be here right now. We wouldn't have made it."

"You came into this family for a reason," Maggie added.

Jayden felt his cheeks grow warm — more from the compliments than the spicy chili. He looked down and shrugged. Even though his new family had told him such things before over the past few days, it still made him feel sort of bashful.

"And look how good my head healed!" Rory said, pointing at the scabbed over gash on his forehead. "The doctor said it wouldn't even leave a scar. You did a good job putting the bandage on." He frowned slightly, like he was suddenly disappointed. "Though it would have been kind of cool to have a scar. Like Harry Potter."

Everyone laughed, and then Connor got up and took the last cookie that sat on a plate on the kitchen counter.

"Hey, I was going to eat that! No fair. You had, like, three this morning before we went snowmobiling!" Maggie yelled.

Connor stuffed it in his mouth and sat back down at the table.

"Dad!" Maggie wailed.

"Okay, Connor had the last cookie, but you get first dibs on the radio on the way home," Mr. Walcott announced. "How does that sound?"

Maggie beamed and Connor started to protest, but all that came out was muffled gobbledygook because his mouth was stuffed with cookie.

Jayden looked around the table. As the good-natured bantering continued, a huge smile lit up his face. He felt really glad the Walcotts had invited him into their family. Yes, he was different from them in many ways, but somehow after all they'd been through together, the differences didn't matter so much. He complemented the family in his own way. And he felt more and more comfortable with them with each passing day. Even when they bickered over silly things like the last cookie. He hoped with all his heart that he would be with the Walcotts for a long, long time.

All too soon, they'd locked up the cabin and loaded the last of the bags into the new van.

"We aren't expecting any snow on the way home are we?" Maggie asked as she swung open the sliding door and climbed inside.

"No, thank goodness!" Mr. Walcott said. "It's supposed to be fair weather all the way home."

As Jayden buckled himself in, Mr. Walcott turned to him and said, "Next time we come up here, it'll be early summer and a totally different experience. There'll be boating, swimming, fishing, and cookouts. Mom will be coming along." He grinned. "And I promise you won't be caught in a blizzard. How does that sound?"

"Perfect," Jayden said. And it was. As long as he was with the Walcotts, he was ready for any adventure headed his way.

More About BLIZZARDS

According the US National Weather Service, a blizzard is a snowstorm with winds of at least 35 miles per hour and visibility of less than 1/4 mile lasting for 3 hours or more. However, the term is commonly used for any heavy snowstorm accompanied by strong winds.

Blizzards that form along the East Coast from the mid-Atlantic region up to New England are called nor'easters. These storms move slowly, have incredibly strong winds, and can dump enormous amounts of snow over the region.

The most snow to fall in any 24-hour period happened in Silver Lake, Colorado. Its record-setting snowstorm of 75.8 inches began on April 14, 1921. The blizzard continued well into the next day, ultimately leaving 95 inches of fresh snow on the ground.

The year 1978 was famous for blizzards. Ohio, Michigan, and Indiana were blasted by a storm called the Cleveland Superbomb. Wind gusts approached 100 miles per hour, temperatures dipped below -50°F degrees, and snowdrifts reached 25 feet high. National Guard helicopters flew 2,700 missions to rescue stranded motorists. Doctors and emergency personnel were forced to use skis and snowmobiles. Weeks later, the New England Blizzard of '78 struck, dumping 4 feet of snow on parts of Massachusetts, Rhode Island, and Connecticut. Incredibly strong winds pushed ocean water onto the shore and caused severe coastal flooding, destroying nearly 2,000 homes.

Though many wild animals can survive blizzards, squirrels and quails have trouble finding their buried stashes of food. Domestic animals are also in danger if they can't find shelter. In early October 2013, for example, a rogue blizzard caught cattle ranchers in Nebraska, South Dakota, and Wyoming by surprise. Because they had not yet moved their livestock from summer pastures to more sheltered areas, close to 100,000 head of cattle were lost.

However, not all animals suffer during blizzard conditions. Mice, shrews, and voles keep cozy in tunnels and insulated areas under snow-covered vegetation. And Emperor Penguins can handle wind chills as cold as -76°F degrees and swirling blizzards of 124 miles-per-hour!

If a blizzard or winter storm is in the forecast, here are a few things you can do to stay safe:

- Stay inside. Wind, ice, and snow can bring down power lines, so make sure that your parents have on hand candles; matches or lighters; a battery operated radio; emergency food supplies; and warm blankets.

- Don't travel during a blizzard. But if you do get stranded in a car during a snowstorm, make sure you have plenty of warm clothing and packaged snack foods. And since snow can block the exhaust pipe and fill the car with deadly fumes, leave one window cracked.

- If you get caught outdoors, stay hydrated and nourished so you won't get hypothermia. Move around to keep your blood flowing. If your clothes are wet, try to start a fire to dry them. Create a snow cave or find a sheltered area to block winds. And don't eat snow — it'll only make you colder!

Ready for another thrilling adventure?

Read on for a sneak peek at

VOLCANO BLAST . . .

Noah looked toward the summit of the volcano. It seemed peaceful under the blue skies, but he turned toward his sister for reassurance anyway. "It's not going to erupt, is it?" he yelled over the roar.

"I don't know, but I'm not sticking around to find out!" Emma yelled back. "We need to head back to the boat."

"I'm with you. This is freaking me out. I've never heard anything like it before!" Alex said.

They scrambled down the mountainside as best they could, the scary-loud rumbling sound chasing after them. But it was slowgoing. Painfully slow. Running down the uneven, sloping ground was next to impossible.

"Dad said this volcano might not blow for a hundred years," Noah called out to the other two in ragged huffs. "Maybe thousands."

"In other words, it's totally unpredictable!" Emma barked back. "We can't take any chances. There's no telling how dangerous it may be!"

But Noah wasn't listening anymore. Because just then, he lost his footing on the rough terrain, fell to the ground, and slid down the slope feetfirst. His body twisted, and his stomach scraped the ground as he skidded farther down the slope. Rocks ripped at his jacket, and he clawed at everything he could to stop his momentum.

Finally he slowed enough to struggle back to his feet. He looked up the mountainside to where they'd just come from and stood paralyzed for a moment, not quite believing what he saw. "Guys! Stop! Look!" he screamed.

A deep vertical crack in the earth was cleaving the ground before his eyes. Steam and smoke sprang from the crack, which expanded quickly, snaking down toward them.

The other two stopped in their tracks and turned to see what Noah was screaming about.

"It's a fissure," Emma shouted. "And it'll make its way to us in a matter of seconds. We need to keep going! It could start spewing lava!"

As they hustled toward the shoreline, which still seemed impossibly far off, Noah kept glancing behind them. The fissure seemed to be catching up. It was spreading faster than they could run.

Maybe we should be running sideways to escape it, Noah thought. But by that time, they'd reached a dip in the slope that suddenly deepened and narrowed — a natural crevice that had formed years ago. They'd have to climb up a steep embankment to go sideways, which would take too much time.

"Hurry!" Alex screamed at the twins.

But Noah couldn't help craning his neck to look at the rift again. Lava was already spraying into the air where it'd first opened up. And just feet behind them, the earth continued to crack open. "It caught us!

Jump to the side! Jump to the side!" Noah bellowed.

Alex and Emma jumped to the right. Noah jumped to the left. In an instant they were separated by the fissure, which had split the earth between them.

They couldn't continue the way they'd been going. The crack was too close. And there was no telling when lava and gases would come pouring out of it.

Noah watched as Alex, in a move like Spider-Man, climbed up the steep incline on his side of the crevice. He waited at the top for Emma to follow. But Emma was tiny and not athletic at all. She kept slipping as she tried to claw her way up. Noah watched helplessly as Alex knelt down with his hand extended, trying to pull Emma up. But she couldn't reach his hand.

Steam started to rise from the opening, and Noah knew his best chance to reach the shoreline was to climb up his side of the crevice and get as far away as possible. Still, he remained frozen in place, watching his sister struggle.

Emma spun around and looked at him. "Go," she shrieked. "Just go. Don't worry about me."

By now molten lava gushed from all along the fissure, a glowing serpent racing toward them. But Noah couldn't leave Emma behind. He wouldn't. On instinct, he got a running start and leapt over the deep split in the earth that held a cauldron of boiling lava. Lava ready to spew up and incinerate anything in its way . . .

As Noah landed his giant leap, he heard an ominous hiss and felt a warning wave of heat at his back. He wrapped his arms around Emma and lifted her toward Alex's outstretched hand.

"Almost. Just another inch!" Alex yelled.

Noah strained and grunted until Alex finally got a good grip on her hand. Alex pulled as Emma dug into the earth with her feet, desperately trying to get some traction. The next few seconds seemed to last forever, but eventually she managed to clamber up the side of the crevice, and Noah scurried up after her.

They'd made it just in time. Lava violently shot up from the opening, splattering all around them like a fiery orange hailstorm. Poisonous gases began to fill the air, and they coughed and sputtered but wasted no time stumbling over the rugged terrain away from the lava and its venomous show of force.

Noah had seen lava at Kilauea plenty of times before, but it'd been nothing like this! Visitors were always kept a safe distance away from the stable eruptions. His dad was one of the select few allowed past the barriers. Sometimes he'd even don a fireproof suit and collect lava from trails that oozed at a snail's pace. But even his dad wouldn't mess around with a fast-moving fissure like the one they'd just escaped!

With pounding hearts driving them onward, the kids ran at full speed until Emma stopped to catch her breath a good fifteen minutes later. She bent over, hands on her knees. "We should be safe now," she panted. "Fissures aren't as explosive as when the summit blows. We should be far enough away now to be okay."

As Emma talked, Noah noticed his arm was stinging. The front of his jacket had ripped when he fell, and now it had a quarter-sized burn on the sleeve. A blob of lava must have singed its way through the jacket. His shirt sleeve was intact, but the intensity of the heat still managed to burn his arm. It hurt, but he knew it could've been so, so much worse. Silly with relief, he couldn't help but crack a joke. "First time I've worn this jacket. Ruined already."

"Yeah, wait until Dad sees it. You're going to get in so much trouble!" Emma played along. She'd finally caught her breath, and now she stood up straight. "Thanks, Noah." She walked over and hugged her twin.

They bickered a lot, being so different, so it was something she didn't do often and it caught Noah off guard.

"It was truly stupid of you to try to rescue me, but I'm awful glad you did," she said.

Noah grinned and hugged her back. He

was glad, too. He couldn't have lived with himself if he'd left her.

"Thanks for pulling me up, too, Alex," Emma said, pulling away from her brother. "You're brave. You could've left us both in the dust. And I'd be toast right about now."

The volcano's rumbling seemed quieter . . . for now. "We should probably go down to the boat and meet up with Dad," Noah said, looking around. He frowned. "But which way do we go to get back to the boat?"

Emma crooked her neck in both directions, and Noah grew concerned. What if they were lost? Dad was probably already waiting for them and he'd be worried.

"We ran straight down from the eagle's nest, then veered to the right when the fissure caught up to us." Alex took his compass out of his pocket and looked at it, then squinted toward the coastline in the distance. "If we head down from here, I think we should be near the boat."

Suddenly the volcano's constant grumbling grew louder. The earth shook once again, with much more force than before. But before Noah could wrap his mind around what was happening —

BOOM!

An ear-shattering explosion rocked the earth and blackened the sky.

The bright sunshine disappeared. Instinctively Noah looked toward the top of the mountain. Instead of the usual trail of white puffy smoke coming from the summit, a dark expanding mushroom-shaped ash cloud loomed overhead.

For a second, Noah, Emma, and Alex remained still, spellbound at the sight.

Then a large smoldering chunk of rock came hurtling toward them, landing with a loud crash only feet away from where they were standing.

Emma screamed. "That could have hit us!"

"We need to get out of here!" Noah urged. "Right now!"

"But where?" Emma looked at Noah, her eyes desperate. "There's nowhere to go!"

Bits and pieces of what was once the top of the inside of the crater began to rain down on them.

"Over here!" Alex called. "Quick!"

Noah and Emma followed him, holding their hands over their heads to protect themselves from falling debris.

Alex led them to a small cave similar to the one Noah had peeked inside earlier. The opening of this one was narrow, with room for only one person to crawl inside at a time.

Alex shooed Emma inside first and waited for Noah to follow her before scuttling in himself.

Past the small opening, the cave widened. It was about five feet high, ten feet wide, and not deep at all. The kids huddled on the cold, damp ground and listened to the sky falling outside. Noah knew there was nothing to do but get used to their new surroundings. Only he didn't like the thought of being stuck in the cave. He was starting to feel claustrophobic.

"So how long do we stay in here? Are we safe?" Noah asked Emma. For once he was glad his sister was a know-it-all. She always took an interest in the science of volcanoes, just like their dad, so out of the three of them he figured that made her the expert.

In the dimness of the small cave, Emma pushed at the bent plastic frames of her glasses, trying to straighten them without much success. "Safer than being outside," Emma said. "We need to stay put until the rocks from the blast stop falling. But we can't stay here for long. Flows of lava could be headed our way. Or worse, a sudden mudslide."

Noah shuddered at the thought of being entombed by lava or mud. Sealed up for eternity, never to be found. It didn't help his feeling of claustrophobia. "I hate volcanoes," he said. "They're terrible."

Even in the scenario they found themselves in, Emma couldn't resist. "That's true. But they're also responsible for creating eighty percent of the land in the world. There would be no Hawaii if it weren't for volcanoes erupting," Emma said. "And they make the soil rich for farming. So there's a bright side."

Before Noah could get exasperated at her, Alex exclaimed, "A bright side for us? Right now?"

"Nope. For us, volcanoes stink. Big-time," she admitted. After that, there was nothing much left to say, and the kids settled into an uncomfortable silence.

After a while, the chatter of falling rocks seemed to fade. When Noah peeked through the opening of the cave, he saw only delicate ash drifting down like a gentle snowfall.

"I think it's time to get going," Alex said. He started for the opening, but Emma grabbed him. "Wait."

"Why?" Noah asked. He was anxious to get out of the cramped cave, too.

"It's dangerous to breathe in the ash that's coming down," she said.

"Yeah, but it's better than being buried alive in here," Noah replied.